I0209508

SO CLEARLY BEAUTIFUL

So Clearly Beautiful

A Poetry Collection

by

DARREN C. DEMAREE

BOOKS

Adelaide Books
New York/Lisbon
2019

SO CLEARLY BEAUTIFUL
A Poetry Collection
By Darren C. Demaree

Copyright © by Darren C. Demaree
Cover design © 2019 Adelaide Books

Published by Adelaide Books, New York / Lisbon
adelaidebooks.org
Editor-in-Chief
Stevan V. Nikolic

All rights reserved. No part of this book may be reproduced in any
manner whatsoever without written permission from the author except in
the case of brief quotations embodied in critical articles and reviews.

For any information, please address Adelaide Books
at info@adelaidebooks.org
or write to:
Adelaide Books
244 Fifth Ave. Suite D27
New York, NY, 10001

ISBN-13: 978-1-951214-79-1

Printed in the United States of America

This book is dedicated to Isabelle and Thomas.

Contents

The Moon Is Too Big To Be The Moon

Our bodies have fathers
& yet, on the clearest nights
it appears

we all had nine mothers
& a voice they ignored
in the distance.

Some midnights
have a violent clarity
& the first one

your first child survives
will churn up
the sky for many years.

The Sky Is All Of The Colors

Once a child knows anything,
a child knows everything
& that first burst

is a torrent, is an attitude,
is a music expressed
every moment of the day

& if they find their good blood
rising amidst the removal
of the shadows,

they will devastate
even the smallest silence
with a *did you know*

or a *well, I learned that*
& all you can do is roll over
& tell them that it's five

in the morning right now
& the shortest wave lengths
of blue have yet to find

any of us quite yet.
They will rock back
& forth, cross-legged

& then they will turn on
all of the lights in the house
in preparation for the day.

What We Hang From The Roof Of Our House

All of it, from the flags
to the planters
to the hosing

that connects
to our rain barrel
is meant

to be swung from
like our house
is a pirate ship.

I refuse
to have it
any other way.

We go to the hospital
when we need to,
but it's never quiet

& it's never quiet
& it's never quiet
& it's never going to be.

Donut Friday #1

How many moons
does the baker grow
& hold before we

know exactly
that all we want
is to consume

their celestial sugars?
Son, I would ask
you more,

but your mouth
is full of Friday's
heaven. You've got

a beard made
entirely of sprinkles,
my blessed son.

Donut Friday #2

In the beginning
of your childhood
you missed

your sister so much
when she went
off to school

in the morning
I needed a child-
hood that could

that could trump
your bird-screaming
sadness. I choose

sugar. Your love
was for sale
& I wanted it

& once a week,
I spend seven dollars
to position us

at the window
at Buckeye Donut,
so that we can spit

crumbs at the world
& know the world
continued anyway.

Donut Friday #3

If we wore shirts
with collars on them
they would be caked

in chocolate crème
& powdered sugar
& all of the jelly.

We dress down
to the donut's level,
because we know

who we are
& besides, staining
t-shirts together

is the same thing
as writing
down our history.

Donut Friday #8

We don't sit quietly.
We don't eat quietly.
We leave crumbs.

Donut Friday #15

Last year, we spent four hundred
& sixty-two dollars on donuts.
We had refinanced the house

at a lower rate, so we saved close
to that amount. I am among
the best of all of the adults.

Donut Friday #16

Parting near
the prow
of the weekend,

Thomas becomes
the satellite
& the pole

that swings it
around my planet
& those quick

breaths I take
to follow him
around Columbus

make me
a different kind
of an aging ship.

I have no fear of ice.
I have no fear
of being lost

with my son.
We shuttle every
shake together.

Donut Friday #19

Some light
you can hold
in your hands

& place
in your mouth
& make great

promises with.
Some light
dissolves inside

of you. I want
so badly
for that

to mean
something more
than it does.

Donut Friday #28

Unrestrained
splendor
& the ability

to buy it cheaply.
This part
of the world is good

& easy. It can
even come with
sprinkles.

Donut Friday #31

One open box
& a blanket
in the dew

of the Park
of Roses,
Thomas

& I watch
the workers
ready the fields

for a whole
weekend's worth
of games

& when they
are done mowing
we offer them

the unopened box
of donuts
we brought

for them.
I always admired
their arboreal

ballet. They deserve
some chocolate crèmes
from Honey Dip.

Donut Friday #33

I built a clock
out of donuts
& it worked

beautifully
for five minutes.
The jelly

& the cinnamon
got warm
& wrapped

a fist around
the gears. Donuts
are good like that.

Donut Friday #37

I saw a man
walking to
a town

that made
wooden docks
& I saw that

man turn
around to follow
me to a town

that made boats.
We were both
imagining

different lives
& it didn't matter
that I was

headed somewhere
to buy donuts.
It gave us

both an hour
to breathe
the sweetness

that comes
with making
any choice at all.

Donut Friday #42

Sugar drunk, I remember
how often I used to be high
or whiskey drunk

before my son was born
& I know that this cute
tradition of us

venturing out into Columbus
every Friday is different
than all of that, but I also

know that I could never, ever
relapse on a Thursday night,
because what if I slept

through a morning
of Donut Friday? I've
invented many traditions

in our family,
just to stay sober,
to remove the randomness

& questioning
& entitlement I feel
while in the trappings

of this dangerous
& darling & methodical
& tempting world.

Donut Friday #44

The morning captures
what the night cannot
& since the best bakeries

close before the sun
descends, we must race
the new world

to the ticket counter.
I have been number one
at Resch's! I keep that

ticket stub in my wallet,
next to the pictures
of my wife, my children

& I tell that story
the same way I tell my
old baseball stories.

Donut Friday #45

Some blossoms need
a little powdered sugar.

Donut Friday #48

If I put a donut
on each of my fingers
& I raise my arms

over my head
& make bear sounds,
I can get Thomas

to laugh so hard
that orange juice
comes out of his nose.

I only attempt this
every three months
or so. Orange juice

is too expensive
& it stains all of his
t-shirts. I want to

make just enough
money, so that I can
afford to be

a donut-loving bear
every Friday. That's
my idea of heaven.

Donut Friday #57

Blue-coated
& wild,
we work our way

through the park-
ing lot of Honey
Dip, we clench

to make it
through the snow
& inside,

all of the tables
are full. We are
not the only ones.

Donut Friday #60

The mist
from the edge
of our weekend

is made up
entirely of
powdered sugar.

Follow me
to the warm,
waiting world!

The Pond Is A Legend, The Pond Creates Legends

We're all running
because of the regard
we have for the waves

that chase us from day
to day, but oh how
it feels like freedom

to have the water offer
itself to us like a bosom.
We are daring

in the context
of a well-placed pond.
The whole family

gets naked
& swims naked
& leaps to pose

in the sun naked
as if we had become
the reason for the sun.

As I Explain Painting

My son is punching
what he painted
& I swear to you,
he's making it better.
What was a blue circle
has been caved in
& what he called
his picture of a strong
boy appears to be
on the edge of a vortex
he cannot help
but become victim to.
This is not how I would
have painted it, but I'm
pretty sure he just
figured out how to do
things differently than
his sister. She's mortified
he ruined the blue circle.
That makes him happy.
I need to buy him
a lot more canvasses.

Here We Are, Sore

We chased those butterflies
for miles, Belle says
& I can't believe I caught one,
Belle says quietly
& I can't believe I tore one
wing off, Belle whispers
& then there is silence for
a while. There are a hundred
butterflies in the field
we are sitting in, but Belle
can only look at the one
still unable to leave her palm.
I tell her to look up into the sky
& to watch all of the butterflies
& that I can fix the injured wing
& as I count down to swing
my arm quickly upward, Belle
sees all of the butterflies
& she sees the butterfly she hurt
rejoining the pattern. Daddy,
Belle says, you fixed her wing
& I don't tell her any different
& I don't open up my fist
until I'm alone again, until
I can wash my hands of her
slight crime, of her panic
& excitement, of my terrible
decision to free her from that.

Sparkler #1

Initially a button,
a spark waiting
for a finger's kiss

to release the lion
in the bee that
hisses to roar

& though it never
gives more, they
can always spell

their names before
the darkness returns
to their hands.

Sparkler #2

There is a part
of childhood
where you learn

everything,
including fire
with your mouth.

If only we could
see that glow
all the way

down, inside
the belly
of curiosity,

but that idea
never makes it
past our teeth.

Sparkler #6

The pond reaches up
from its' reflection
& since we hold

the fire the water
is attempting
to hold, then we

join the war
of the elements.
It would all be

so serious
if the child holding
the sparkler

hadn't gotten naked
after their third
lemonade, if they

hadn't already peed
in the pond. If
they weren't dancing

like a satellite
that's coming close
to losing orbit.

Sparkler #10

Sweetly, the story
continues. The brief fire
confirms our intention

to celebrate to the point
of sacrificing. I could
never dream of making

any real sacrifice
other than my own body.
My children run,

shooting sparks in the air,
declaring their rush
towards a sacrifice

that might continue
their joy. This is why
scars don't haunt us

unless we stop
running in fields
beneath the fireworks.

The world always falls
down around us, but we
get to choose the cascade.

Sparkler #12

Shirt ripped off,
I have so much pride
in my son when he

stuns the crowd
by all of the sudden
being the only chest

bared to the moon.
There's laughter.
There's head shaking.

He folds his fists
into his chest
& smiles as I smile

& then he throws
the cast-off shirt
towards my feet.

The party is his
now. Oh, how much
trouble he'll become

when he figures
out how to un-button
his cargo shorts.

Sparkler #14

Integral to everything,
the children have learned
they cannot hold a dance

long enough to name
a dance. They don't care
about any of that.

Watch how they never
have their balance
long enough to have

such expansionist thoughts.
They are the new Americans.
They hear only the music.

Sparkler #16

Shallow to the leaking
heat, those small hands
are present to pronounce

the ruining of the light
& they never waver,
they never balk

to recover until the last
spark has flown. They
trust the darkness

that is coming. It's in
our bones now, that
though the absence

of glow is a thick forest
in our minds, it's one
we can work our hands in.

Sparkler #21

Without the emperor
of longing,
these children

can exist
almost wholly
in the lighting

of the sparkler.
They carry nothing
into the fire's hold.

Sparkler #22

The best love
is in creating
the ecstatic

nature of each
volley of each
child. Then,

the gift
of not getting
in the way

too often.
There is a cliff.
There is an ocean.

They cannot fly
from one
to the other,

but around other
crop, let them
believe they can.

Sparkler #23

The hole bends
the ankle. The hole
has such confidence

that it exists to be filled
by those small pains
& yet, the children

are flying over it.
I put my face above
the hole. I twist

my neck to lay my ear
to it. I whisper
I love you to the hole

& while I do that
both of the children
climb my back

so that they can echo
my understanding
that holes

always matter so much
more when you don't
acknowledge them.

Sparkler #27

There is no terrifying initiation.
We use controlled fire to light
a controlled burn that has

a dulled handle, but when they run,
streak across the fields with that
slight metal set to burn for a minute

or so, our chests lose a bit of control.
They could be in flight without
knowing how to land, that is how

our chests explain it to us.
They can and they do turn running
with fire into a dance, they spell

their names so the Ohio night
will always remember them,
they fall to the ground once

the fire is gone. The look up at
the sky. Their chests open to swallow
every bit of the world they imagine.

They don't breath right for days.
They smile for a month. They've
claimed something they believe.

The First Profanity

That moment where the bomb
swallows up the atmosphere
after pushing to destroy it all

& that was the imagery
my parents gave me when I was
caught saying *asshole*

& *bitch* when I was seven
& when my child repeated
the line from the pop song

all I felt was a light breeze?
My hair didn't even move
& she looked so happy singing

& as it's not my job to take joy
& show it the lines of a battle
-field, I saved my bullets.

Introducing Cliffs

My children fall down
gently. Even on sidewalks,
the scrapes to cuts

& the blood that follows,
there is hardly any scarring.
My children fall down

gently. Even in waves
they are delivered
to the beach. My children

fall down gently. So,
when the bodies of other
children are on the news

I do not change the channel,
when they talk about death
& it's not the death

of our beloved cat, I leave
the volume high. I will not
frighten my children,

but I cannot stop them
from forming the questions,
from looking at abyss

& feeling that they could
fall forever from that cliff.
I've taught them safety.

I preached some caution.
I've let them hear about
the amount of blood

in the American ocean.
My children fall down
gently. I say it out loud

so that I can hear it
when my worst fears
creep in from the wind.

Not A Leaf, Falls Like A Leaf

     after Derek Walcott

Let the charging
road tar be the whole route
& instead

of us using the pavement,
forcing weight
& wheel on each inch

of the modern path,
let's tell the children
that we are carried by waves

we spent years making,
that the car is lifted
towards home

or the beach. We'll preach
to them to allow
the undulations,

put both hands
outside of the car window
& cup them,

just in case we've chosen
the right day
in the right season

for them to be given
one whole hut
of nature's allowance.

The Pollen Dot

after Helene Johnson

I want my children to breathe
& be brave enough to say
that they were curious enough

to latch themselves to that breathe,
to do good work with that oxygen
& that when they cough,

when they sputter, when they
sneeze to project that breath
back into the world they will have

done so with the knowledge
that though they are as light
as a pollen dot, they are capable

of making a whole world
out of the slight poisons
they have been given.

The Children At The Wedding #1

Celebration of the celebration
& holding all of the rhythms
all at once, the lightning

inside of the art museum
is not always pinned to be
a prize against the static walls;

the lightning, the growl
of the lightning is my children
& they become the whole show

as any dramatic weather
can become the whole show.
There should whole channels

dedicated to my children
where well-dressed people
make hesitant predictions

& look joyful while they do.

The Children At The Wedding #3

Some sons make great art
& some sons punch great art
& both kinds are good at parties.

The Children At The Wedding #7

Beneath the paintings of horses,
my children happen
in a white dress
& in a gray, buttoned vest
& they move as the horses seem
to move in the paintings, in tandem
& yet, diving thought the world
at different speeds. Beneath
the paintings of horses my children
show their bellies to the brush-
strokes, they make faces
at the faces of the animals
& they call, so loudly, so purely
they call to the animals to join them,
to jump out of the paintings
& run the breadth of the buffet.
There are carrots! There are apples!
Beneath the paintings of horses,
my children are peasant children
& they don't want to ride the horses,
they want to run with them forever
& be as free as they can imagine
freedom to be. My children,
my children, I'd follow their voices
with my eyes closed
& on my better days, I do.

The Children At The Wedding #16

Probably a home
in the chaos of good
clothes

& over-ripening
fruit, the sugar
dashed

on everything
& the children
rubbing

their tongues
against all
of that sugar.

The whole mad
parade
of after the vows,

becomes so clearly
beautiful
that it denies

the existence
of the vows
themselves

& makes
a new promise
to the science

of a storm
undeterminable
& beehive at best.

The Children At The Wedding #17

Karate in the dance,
Thomas is the master
of a curious

& wrong history
of our movements.
As a family, we have

no moves, but Thomas
believes quite purely
that you can kick

& spin & never land
& kiss a stranger
on the behind

all in ten seconds.
He is, very much so
my own hero.

The Children At The Wedding #28

The fertility comes from the magic
of the animals

already among us
& it comes from the children

that hope without
hoping, that love in the ecstasy

of being without ever questioning
the soil or occasion.

A child never asks
why we are here, celebrating this?

They dance for the simple reason
that we've given them music.

The Children At The Wedding #29

Without buffering
we hit every wall,
we touched every painting

& as actual art,
we posed every four minutes
when the music stopped.

We reveled in witnesses.
We took pieces
of our clothes off.

I Eliminate The Stick

I could never strike
one of my children
with my own hands,

so I am brisk
in the yard
with the wood

that falls from
our large trees. I
collect it all.

I burn it all.
I extend my bare
arms to my children

when they are awful
& I show them
how the blood

works through
my veins. I show
them my efforts

& that terrifies them.
They balk at
adding more scars.

The Barn Without Color

We all wanted to know
what we would find
in a dilapidated barn

that had lost all red
& all symbol, that had
wood that didn't reach

the ground. All we
found was each other
& enough straw

to sit down for a while.
Our car was broken
down & while we sang

songs waiting
for the tow, more birds
showed up than left

& that is our Ohio.

The Cat's Death Book

Isabelle has been writing
for four months
in a memory journal

we bought her
after Captain died
of kidney failure

& that thin journal
has outlasted
three pencils thus far.

It's incredible. She's
turned their questions
about the animal

into an exploration
of the veil, of what
Captain's body might

have become,
even though she knows
his body was cremated.

It's how delicately
she describes the fire
that consumed

his lifelessness
that is devastating
& how tenderly

in her mind
it *licked his fur clean*
of all that messy death.

It will such a pleasure
to have her write
about my own demise.

In Their Time #1

The fear comes
in not knowing
exactly why
the adults are crying
in the air conditioning
& not knowing why

our bodies curl
from supine to fetal
in the re-positioning
on the couch.
That is the question
in the look

I get from my kids.
Belle can read
the screen
& she knows
how long it takes
her to count

to the height
of the numbers she sees.
Nightly, with the news
she tries to translate
the pictures, the words,
those numbers

& she doesn't have
the language for that.
She's six. She knows
what it means though,
when everyone is crying
at the same time.

In Their Time #2

They want to play
in the waves
without searching
the surf for a change
in color. The pink
would catch

their ankles first.
The red would send
them running.
From the balcony
of the life
they've been given

they would peek
out over the railing
& count the bodies
that washed up
during their games
as practice

to count the new
bodies arriving
in tomorrow's tide.
Children adapt
before they know
why. Those that

can count into
the thousands will
have a place
by this ocean.
Those that can
can create a new

ocean with tender
foam only, will
get to name it.

In Their Time #3

There is light
& there are books.
I've piled them

around my children.
They're researching
the satellites

of our failures.
All of their answers
are questions

we've ignored.
When they turn
five I teach them

how to write
their own books.
I teach them

how to march
forever against
the crushing black.

In Their Time #7

Loaded
& editing
that load,

my kids
make pledges
to people.

I can only
teach them
nine things

& I want
to make sure
seven of them

involve honey
& the promise
to share it.

In Their Time #9

No tree is urgent,
which is why
my children
worship the trees.

In Their Time #10

The overshadows reach,
but cannot touch
the suite

of their futures
& even if their beach
is manmade

& touches no ocean,
the children
will hold the sand

the same way they do
in display of the moon.
They will know

how much breaking
went into that
wonderful texture.

They will rub it
on their cheeks
& let the playfulness

of the water
take it from them
in the natural time.

In Their Time #16

Is this smoke
before or after
the fire?

I'd rather
the young ones
be fighters

than the collectors
& labelers
of the ash.

In Their Time #17

If it's your art's turn
to wear the variety
& push,

then you must
use your chest
& collect as much air

as possible. Children,
you must shout.
If it's not your art's turn,

then you must be gentle
& whisper all of the time.
No. That was your father.

You should shout
even when you have
nothing at all to say,

because if you say nothing
the right way,
that can be art as well.

In Their Time #22

The fullness outside
of the field is tricky.
The reflections lend

only the worship
of the reflections
& to know as a farmer

knows, that it's their
season to work
or their season for crop,

that is guessing
& faith, or just bravado
around this city.

In Their Time #29

The moon assumes the nest,
as do my children
& when the morning comes

& they must sing
to bring the sun closer
to them, they sing too loudly

& it wakes me up.
I should have spent more
time explaining

Greek mythology to them.
I should have told
them they weren't birds.

In Their Time #30

The milk was fine.
I added honey to it.
My children saw that.

Acknowledgements

The most important people in the world are the people that are good to your children. Thank you to everyone who is good to the Demaree kids.

Credits

Bluestem – "Donut Friday #8"
IDK – "Donut Friday #15"
Mayday – "The Children at the Wedding #1" and "The Children at the Wedding #3"
Moonglasses – "The Children at the Wedding #17"
Off the Coast – "The Children at the Wedding #28" and "The Children at the Wedding #29"
Parcel – "The Moon Is Too Big to be the Moon" and "Not A Leaf, Falls Like a Leaf"
Poydras Review – "The Barn Without Color"
Quail Bell – "Donut Friday #19"
Random Sample – "In Their Time #1"
The Round – "Donut Friday #2"
Route 7 Review – "Donut Friday #28"
Scrittura – "Donut Friday #42" and "Donut Friday #44"
The Tribe – "In Their Time #7" and "In Their Time #9"
Unbroken – "Here We Are, Sore"
VerseWrights – "Introducing Cliffs"

About the Author

Darren C. Demaree is from Mount Vernon, Ohio. He is a graduate of the College of Wooster, Miami University, and Kent State University. He is the author of thirteen poetry collections, most recently "So Clearly Beautiful", which was published by Adelaide Books. He is the recipient of a 2018 Ohio Arts Council Individual Excellence Award, the Louis Bogan Award from Trio House Press, and the Nancy Dew Taylor Award from Emrys Journal. He is the Managing Editor of the Best of the Net Anthology and Ovenbird Poetry. He is currently living in Columbus, Ohio with his wife and three children.

www.ingramcontent.com/pod-product-compliance
Lightning Source LLC
Chambersburg PA
CBHW020328090426
42735CB00009B/1453